Someday Saints

America's Blesseds, Venerables, and Servants of God

Father Solanus Casey
Bishop Frederic Baraga
Father Samuel Mazzuchelli

Written and Illustrated by
Laurie J. Schmitt

NIHIL OBSTAT:
    Rev. Jesse D. Burish
    Censor Librorum
    July 6, 2022

IMPRIMATUR:
    +Most Rev. William Patrick Callahan
    July 19, 2022

Copyright 2022
Sancti In Spe Books
www.LaurieSchmitt.com

For my grand prizes,
my very own someday saints.

Love, Grandma

Praise for Someday Saints

"My understanding of holiness changed in college when a friend of mine said, 'There are saints everywhere! There are saints all around us.' By this she meant that many people are living lives of great holiness 'right under our noses.' Since that conversation, I have been more able to recognize how ordinary people, family members, friends, and fellow parishioners are living out their mission from Christ to be 'the salt of the earth.' All the saints, whether recognized by the universal Church or recognized only by a few, are ordinary people who cooperate with God's supernatural grace. Through the lives of three ordinary men from various backgrounds who said 'yes' to God and served Him and His people with great love, *Someday Saints* is a reminder that there are saints all around us. This book will inspire people of all ages to say 'yes' to God and become someday saints in our own time."

-Father Daniel Sedlacek
Parish Priest, La Crosse Diocese, Wisconsin

"With gentle and inviting prose, Laurie Schmitt shares the stories of three "someday saints" in *Someday Saints: America's Blesseds, Venerables, and Servants of God*. While their stories may be little-known, the impact of these men on those they served left a tremendous legacy of faith. By sharing these tales with our youngest "someday saints", we underscore for them and ourselves the unique invitation God gives each of us to love and serve those around us. Inviting!"

-Lisa M. Hendey
Author of *I'm a Saint in the Making*

"*Someday Saints* is an engaging and understandable introduction to the canonization process and a delightful adventure with three someday saints. Children and adults will be drawn by the lyrical storytelling and the beautiful illustrations. This book is a fantastic encouragement to children, emphasizing their own call to holiness and sainthood. A book worthy of Catholic parents' shelves!"

–Olivia Spears
Blog Manager, Blessed Is She

"Beautifully illustrated and joyfully written! Laurie's newest addition to our family's storytime, *Someday Saints*, brings sainthood to life, especially for little ones. Ensuring our faith is tangible is critically important as our children grow to embrace their own spiritual journey. Thank you for yet another resource to teach our children how to live out the will of God and follow the path to sainthood."

-Katie Curran
Creator, Totus Tuus Treasures

"Rarely do children's saint stories move past the basic biography and into the heart of who the person was. Laurie's *Someday Saints* goes beyond the facts, using a warm storytelling style to reveal what mattered most to these historical figures. She uses a connecting theme which shows the vocational path each person followed, teaching us that growing in holiness should be a part of our whole lives. Beginning with their childhood and family life is a perfect way to connect with kids and demonstrate that they, too, are called by God to listen and follow Him. *Someday Saints* is a warm collection inviting children to come to know the holy men and women that have spread the faith throughout America, inspiring us to follow in their footsteps."

-Katie Bogner
Author of *Through the Year with Jesus* and *Through the Year with Mary*

"What a wonderful way to learn about the canonization process as a family, as well as these special *Someday Saints*. I love how canonization prayers are included at the end of each story, inviting children to pray regularly for their new heavenly friends!"

–Katie Warner
Bestselling children's book author, FirstFaithTreasury.com

"Want your children to aspire to holiness? Laurie Schmitt's *Someday Saints* offers a glimpse into the lives of three Christlike men from not-so-long-ago who shone the light of Jesus in the upper Midwest of America. I pray that these stories will inspire all who read and hear them to note how God's providence and love flourishes in our own lives. Humble servants, Blessed Solanus Casey, Venerable Frederic Baraga, and Venerable Samuel Mazzuchelli said "fiat" ("yes") to God's Divine Will. They would have been the first to tell you that they were ordinary men serving our extraordinary God! God willing, we can serve Him, too."

-Marlys Honeyman
Children's book author, *I Am*

"*Someday Saints* is a meaningful way for young children to learn about Father Mazzuchelli and his bringing heaven's treasure to all with whom he ministered."

-Sister Barbara Hubeny, O.P.
Sinsinawa Mound, Wisconsin

"There are so many holy men and women to learn about in history, and Laurie Schmitt does a fantastic job bringing these lesser known men to life. Give your kids great examples of faith with *Someday Saints* – a book that makes it that much easier to live liturgically!"

-Jenna Hines
Author of *The Lazy Liturgical*

Contents

Foreword...Page 7

Are You a Someday Saint?...Page 8

Father Solanus Casey...Page 11
Biography...Page 40
Canonization Prayer...Page 42

Bishop Frederic Baraga...Page 43
Biography...Page 68
Beatification Prayer...Page 70

Father Samuel Mazzuchelli...Page 71
Biography...Page 98
Beatification Prayer...Page 100

Foreword

How does the Lord guide us and encourage us? How does He share His wisdom? How does He show us the path to eternal life? We look to the Church and her teachings, and we know the need for prayer. Certainly, we think of the Sacraments and Sacred Scripture. But we also are drawn to the power of good example, indeed of holy example, and so we are blessed by the Communion of Saints, "the great cloud of witnesses" to Jesus Christ.

Even more wonderful is the witness of a holy life from someone near to us in some way, for example, from our country or from our region. "Someday Saints" introduces us to the powerful example of three holy men who served the Lord and His Church in the upper midwest of the United States. The stories of Bishop Frederic Baraga, Father Solanus Casey and Father Samuel Mazzuchelli will capture young imaginations and foster in young hearts the love of Jesus Christ.

Fr. Paul Check
Executive Director
Shrine of our Lady of Guadalupe
La Crosse, Wisconsin

Are you a Someday Saint?

What does it mean to be a "someday saint?" Simply this, that by living out our baptismal promises, by giving ourselves in service to God and others, by growing in grace, and living lives of virtue, we grow closer to God, which is what it means to become holy. In fact, "saint" comes from "sanctus," the Latin word for "holy." God wants us to be holy, so that someday we may enter Heaven and spend the rest of forever with Him.

The three "someday saints" in this book are on the way to becoming Saints, with a capital "S," through the official process of canonization of the Catholic Church. The process takes time and there are steps along the way, but we can learn from their examples, of how they lived out God's holy call for them. This can help us to become "someday saints," too.

How does someone become a canonized saint in the Catholic Church? First, the official cause is opened for review by a local bishop. Did the person live a life of heroic virtue? The person's life is reviewed, and if the person's holiness is evident, then the cause is confirmed in Rome. At this step, the candidate is granted the title "Servant of God."

Next, the life of the new "Servant of God" is looked at very closely. A person, called a "postulator," is put in charge of collecting all of the necessary facts and presenting these to the Congregation for the Causes of Saints in Rome for review. Once the Congregation approves, the worthy candidate is given the title of "Venerable."

And then? A miracle, granted by God through the intercession of the would-be saint, must be proven. (However, if the holy person died for the faith as a martyr, no miraculous answer to prayer is needed to prove his holiness.) If so, the title of "Blessed" is granted to the candidate.

Finally, after a second miracle is brought about by answered prayer through the saint's intercession, and confirmed by the Congregation, the holy person is granted the title of "Saint" (with a capital "S").

The world needs holy heroes, such as Father Solanus Casey, Bishop Frederic Baraga, and Father Samuel Mazzuchelli. These three "someday saints" promoted the Gospel in the region around the Great Lakes, in Wisconsin, Michigan, and beyond. Father Solanus Casey, a Wisconsin farm boy, milked cows on his family farm, and responded to God's call, becoming a Capuchin. Bishop Frederic Baraga, born in Slovenia, came to the New World as a missionary priest, desiring to reach the indigenous peoples and bring the Gospel message to them. Father Samuel Mazzuchelli, born in Italy, seemed to have the world at his fingertips, and gladly sacrificed it all in order to bring the Gospel of Jesus Christ to the people in North America.

These someday saints overcame obstacles by prayer, fasting, and persevering in their vocations.

Several places in the United States preserve historical artifacts and promote the cause of these holy men, including the Solanus Casey Center in Detroit, Michigan; the Bishop Baraga Association in Marquette, Michigan; and Sinsinawa Dominican Sisters Archives in Sinsinawa, Wisconsin. The Shrine of Our Lady of Guadalupe, in La Crosse, Wisconsin, has a special place which honors their memory as well.

Each man is recognized for his contribution in fostering the faith in the hearts and lives of the people of the upper Midwest region of the United States. Their virtuous lives and heroic example left a mark in America's history through the missions and churches they founded, but more importantly, in the lives of the people they served. Follow the examples of these someday saints, for you are called to be a someday saint, too.

-Laurie J. Schmitt
October 2, 2022
Feast of the Guardian Angels

Walk in, the Door is Open

The Ministry of Blessed Solanus Casey

High on a hill, above the icy Mississippi River, fresh snow swirled in the air. It frosted the trees, and wrapped the frozen farm fields and wintery Wisconsin woods in white.

On this blowing, cold day in November, in a log cabin, cozy and warm, Bernard Francis Casey was born.

Papa, knocking on the bedroom door, asked, "Mama, can we come in?"

Behind him, five little faces were sneaking a peek at their baby brother, Barney. Mama laughed.

"Yes. Walk in, the door is open."

Fresh fallen snow swished as the horse-drawn sleigh slid on its way to St. Joseph's Church.

"Barney is ready for baptism!" the children squealed, scurrying to get in from the chill.

The priest stepped aside, saying,

"There's always room in the family of God. Walk in, the door is open."

"Our family keeps growing," Papa said.
"Let's move to a bigger farm.
There's one not too far away."

On moving day, Barney and his brothers
helped haul things into their new home.

Mama met them, saying,

"Thank you!
Walk in, the door is open."

Barney and his brothers
got right to work,
milking the cows
and plowing the fields.
When the work was done,
they rambled in the woods,
fished, and made wishes
on the banks of the
Trimbelle River.

One hot dry day, Mama hollered, "Children! A grass fire! Sprinkle holy water and prayers all around!" Fire gobbled up the barn, but the family was safe and the house and crops were spared. Neighbors came running.

"Are you okay?" they shouted.

Mama met them on the stoop, saying,

"I've found a new farm," Papa said, hugging Mama. "Railroad tracks run through it leading to St. Patrick's Parish."

Mama smiled, saying, "Barney can make his First Holy Communion there."

Barney knelt in the church, wondering, "When the time is right, I might ask if there's room for me at God's altar."

He heard a whisper, saying,

"There's a special place for you. Walk in, the door is open."

As he grew older, Barney worked at the lumber mill and a prison, too.

A new streetcar came to the busy town of Stillwater, and he hopped right in the driver's seat.

On the cobblestone streets, people stopped and stepped up for a ride. He'd say with a grin, "Welcome aboard. Walk in, the door is open."

Barney's streetcar driving took him to the thriving town of Superior. The town was busy with shipbuilders and rough rowdy sailors, loud lumbermen, and cumbersome railways hauling grain, coal, and ore.

In this noisy place, he heard the message loud and clear,

"Go to Detroit. Walk in, the door is open."

Not wasting any time,
he traveled by train
in a blistering blizzard
to St. Bonaventure Friary.

Shivering on Christmas Eve,
he trudged through the snow
to the monastery door.

One of the friars shouted,

"It's cold out there! Walk in, the door is open."

"Father Solanus," the Brothers told him, "you are the new doorkeeper."

It did not take long before visitors came to chat with him. Mothers and fathers desired prayers for their children. Working men and women were wrung out with worry. No matter what the troubles were, each one wanted to tell Solanus.

His monastery brothers were busy trying to get their own work done, and the doorbell's buzz was a bother.

"I know what to do," Solanus said, nailing a sign on the friary door. The statement was plain:

"Walk in, the door is open."

Solanus jotted down each person's needs into a book. Then he marked on the page, "Thanks be to God!" when prayers were answered.

His healing ministry grew as he nourished souls. So many miracles happened that soon he had bundles of books FILLED with answered prayers.

A married couple came blaming each other, but deep down inside they wanted to be happy.

"Father Solanus, pray for us, that we may have peace of heart!"

Solanus bowed his head, and simply said,

"Love is worth fighting for. Walk in, the door is open."

One day while he was writing, he looked up to see a sad man standing on the threshold.

"I'm worried," he explained, "the doctor has given me bad news. If something happens to me, who will take care of my children?"

Solanus welcomed him in. Comforting him, he said,

"Tell me about it. Walk in, the door is open."

A mom and dad came through the door, carrying their child, crippled with polio. Solanus bent with listening ears as glistening tears rolled down his cheeks.

"Have faith. Let the healing enter in," he told them. He winked at the boy, calling to him, "Come."

The child wriggled away from his mom and went running to Solanus' open arms!

"Believe and receive. Walk in, the door is open."

One hundred poor men packed the
dining room, hungry for bread.
"There's none to be had,
but join me in praying," Solanus said.

"Our Father who art in heaven, hallowed be Thy name. Thy kingdom come, Thy will be done, on earth as it is in heaven. Give us this day, our daily bread—"

"Would you like some bread?" a delivery man interrupted, poking his head in. "I've got a truck full!" Solanus raised his hands to heaven, rejoicing,

"Thanks be to God! Walk in, the door is open!"

A bumbling, grumbling guy stumbled in bellowing, "Where's that Solanus fella? I'd like to pop him on the nose!"

"Is that so?" Solanus asked. "What's the problem?"

"He has my mother crying about me and my rotten life. She keeps praying and telling me, 'Go talk to Solanus.' So I'm here to talk!" he yelled, with his fists swinging in the air.

"I am he," Solanus nodded, and listened to what the man had to say. After a little while, the man was listening to Solanus. No longer angry, the rough man smiled as the priest walked with him outside.

Solanus smiled back at him,

"Come back anytime. Walk in, the door is open."

Blessed André Bessette came from Canada, just to ask for Solanus' blessing! The two holy porters, these gatekeepers of glory, grinned at each other and bowed. Neither knew the language of the other, but the message was clear. Since one spoke French, and the other English, they prayed in Latin, the language of the Church.

"In nomine Patris, et Filii, et Spiritus Sancti. Amen."

Blessed André knelt for his blessing from Solanus, and Solanus knelt for his next.

"Walk in, the door is open."

The hot summer sun, streaming through the door, splashed sparkling flashes around his room. Solanus lay in the hospital bed. Glad of heart, he said, "I've given back all that's been given to me. There's just one thing more! I give my soul to Jesus Christ."

Angel wings fluttered in the sun's beaming rays, and he heard a voice sweetly say,

"Heaven's gate waits for you. Walk in, the door is open."

Biography of Bernard Solanus Casey

Blessed Solanus Casey, a humble Capuchin porter, blessed the lives of those who came to the door of the monastery. With a joyful heart and a listening ear, he shared spiritual counsel and genuine friendship with his visitors, becoming so popular that people flooded the friary to talk with him. The line outside the door seemed to have no end, and the friars became annoyed with the doorbell's incessant ringing. A sign was finally posted on the door that simply read, "Walk In."

Solanus' personal life experiences made him very approachable. In 1870, he was born to Irish immigrant parents on a farm in western Wisconsin. His parents fought hard to provide for their growing family through times of economic hardship, crop failure, and family loss. When Solanus was a young boy, two of his sisters died from diphtheria; the illness left him with a soft, wispy sounding voice. Even so, many came to hear what he had to say for his words brought grace and healing.

As a farm boy, he milked cows, helped with field work and other chores, and did his schooling whenever he was able. As a teenager, he held various jobs, for a time working as a logger, a prison guard, and a streetcar operator.

Solanus had a great devotion to the Blessed Virgin Mary, donned the brown scapular, and daily prayed the rosary. Through his novena prayer, specifically asking for direction in his vocation, he clearly heard the answer, "Go to Detroit." Within a few weeks, his life as a Capuchin had begun.

He struggled with the academics of seminary life, eventually being ordained as simplex priest in 1904. His humble beginnings in the rural countryside prepared him to serve God in big cities such as Detroit, Harlem, and New York City.

Through his mission as door keeper, he counseled the broken hearted, healed the sick, and prophesied to those in need of spiritual vision. While at Saint Bonaventure's in Detroit, in the years after the economic crash of 1929, Solanus established a soup kitchen to feed the hungry and encourage the downcast. This was the first of its kind and is still in operation today.

Thousands of miracles were recorded, handwritten in his books and prayed for by Solanus. "Thanks be to God" penned in the margins, was the humble porter's response to these answered prayers. In May 2017, Solanus was named "Blessed" by Pope Francis.

Prayer for the Canonization of Blessed Solanus Casey, OFM Cap.

O God, I adore You.
I give myself to You.
May I be the person
You want me to be,
and may Your will be done
in my life today.
I thank You for the gifts
You gave Father Solanus.
If it is Your Will,
bless us with the canonization
of Father Solanus
so that others may imitate
and carry on his love
for all the poor
and suffering of our world.
As he joyfully accepted Your divine plans,
I ask You, according to Your Will,
to hear my prayer for...
(state your intention)
through Jesus Christ our Lord.
Amen.

To report favors granted,
visit solanuscasey.org

Or contact:
Cause for Canonization of Blessed Solanus Casey
1780 Mt. Elliott Street
Detroit, MI 48207
(313) 579-2100

Frederic's Feet

The Missionary Travels of Venerable Bishop Baraga

Frederic sat on the dry, dusty roadside, in the deep valley of Dobernice, in his homeland of Slovenia. Beneath the peaks of the Alps, he rubbed his aching feet. They were blistered and bruised, swollen and sore, because he had given another pair of his shoes away.

The parish priest passed him on the road. "Dear Frederic, you are destined for great things,

but how will you get there?"

"By my bare feet."

When Frederic was older he went to the University in Vienna. He studied law and learned different languages. On vacations he crisscrossed the countryside, wading through rivers and hiking over hills.

At the top of the mountain, he marveled at the wonderful world God had made. "I'm going to be a priest someday," he told his friends.

"How will you get there?"

"By prayer and study."

Young Father Frederic, newly ordained, loved the folks of his homeland, but he had a grand dream to be a missionary, to serve people in a faraway place. Father Frederic visited his family to say good bye.

"I long for the mission fields of North America," he told them.

"But how will you get there?"

"By sailing on a steamship."

Father Frederic entered New York Harbor and trekked across the Appalachian Mountains to meet Bishop Fenwick in Cincinnati. There he studied the ways and the words of the Ottawa tribe.

In the spring he said, "I'm off to see the people of the wild north woods."

The bishop asked,

"But how will you get there?"

"By riding on horseback."

Angelus bells chimed good morning from the log cabin church in Arbor Croche, as the people gathered inside for Mass. In the evening twilight, they came again to sing and pray.

Father Frederic, busy with services and schooling the children, made time to write the first prayer book in the Ottawa language. One day he announced, "Many others must hear the Gospel message, so it's time I visit new places."

"But how will you get there?"

"In soft-soled moccasins, by way of the woodland trails."

He made his way, hiking past deer in the shady forest. Chattering squirrels bounced from branch to branch, leading him to his new mission at Grand River.

Father Frederic built a church, school, and house, but it wasn't long before he learned of an island set in the cool blue waters of Lake Superior.

"Madeline Island," he mused, "it's time I visit the village of La Pointe."

They asked,

"But Father, how will you get there?"

"On the schooner, John Jacob Astor."

All of the people there helped to build a sturdy log church for their new priest.

One day the bells rang loud, sounding out the awful news! A terrible sickness had taken hold of people in a village across the water.

Father Frederic wasted no time. "Let's go, Louis!" he shouted to his friend, as he raced to the boats.

Louis paddled the birch bark canoe out onto the big lake, against the mighty wind. Choppy waves leapt up and around on every side.

"Father! The storm is getting worse and we've got to make it to the shore!" He cried,

"But how will we get there?"

"With confidence and courage."

Whitecaps bounced the little craft up and down as it sailed over the crashing surf and settled on the sandy beach.

"Thanks be to God!" they exclaimed, building a rough wooden cross to mark the spot.

Father Frederic rushed to the little village, and blessed a poor sick woman. "Let the angels carry her to heaven," he said to those standing near. They asked,

"But how will she get there?"

"With the sweetness of sacramental graces."

Father Frederic prayed before dawn each day, kneeling in the village church or on the ground in the forest.

"It's time I visit L'anse," he announced, "I'm the only priest for hundreds of miles!"

His people asked,

"But how will you get there?"

"By following the sun's haloed rays."

He came to the busy mining town, and soon a church and school were built.

"Father Frederic," a messenger cried, "a sick child needs baptism, but he's fifty-seven miles away!" His people asked,

"But how will you get there?"

"Across the cold country by snowshoe."

One day, Father Frederic and his friend Basil set out on foot for Ontonagon River, but instead of following the snowy shoreline, they moved straight across the frozen crust of Lake Superior.

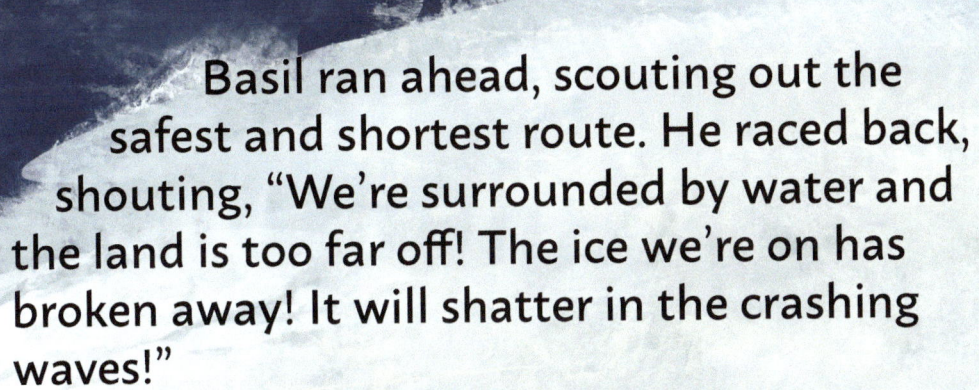

Basil ran ahead, scouting out the safest and shortest route. He raced back, shouting, "We're surrounded by water and the land is too far off! The ice we're on has broken away! It will shatter in the crashing waves!"

"Don't worry," Father Frederic said, "we'll arrive safe and sound." Basil asked,

"But how will we get there?"

"Floating on this raft of ice."

In early spring, Father Frederic set out to see Archbishop Purcell with a satchel packed with pages of his translations and writings. It was a dictionary of words and grammar of the Chippewa people. The first part of the trip was made with a dog sled team. When they came to frozen Lake Huron, they climbed aboard a pony sleigh, which slid them across the lake.

But as the ponies pulled, the ice shattered like glass beneath their hooves!

The sleigh, the ponies, the gear, and every man was plunged into the frigid water. For hours they worked to get the ponies up and out, back onto the thick ice. The men shivered in their frozen clothes.

"Let's move on before we freeze to death!" Father Frederic said through his chattering teeth. The crewmen asked,

"But how will we get there?"

"By walking with hope-filled hurry."

At the Archbishop's house,
Father Frederic laid his papers out to dry.
He had spent years of hard work on his book,
and he didn't want to lose one word of it.

The Archbishop came to him proclaiming,
"You are now Bishop Frederic Baraga
of the rugged north territory and the
land around the big lake. You'll have
thousands of miles to cover," he said,

"but how will you get there?"

"Through the snow
by the glow
of the Northern lights."

Bishop Baraga snowshoed over the cold white terrain beneath the star-speckled sky and through the bitter blizzards of dead winter time.

Timberwolves howled and snowy white owls hooted at his soft shuffling sounds.

In the summertime, canoes carried him on winds and waves that blew fresh and fierce above the wide open lake. He walked in the rain when the weather was warm and wet.

To be in the center of his diocese, he moved from Sault Sainte Marie to Marquette.

He said to his friend, "Now I must attend the Second Baltimore Council." His friend asked,

"But how will you get there?"

"By the round, rolling wheels of a stagecoach."

In Baltimore, Bishop Baraga became very ill. He suspected that the other bishops would not let him go back to the white, wintery north.

"Father Honoratus," he begged, "please, help me return home to Marquette."

His friend asked,

"But how will you get there?"

"With the whistle blowing sound of a railway train."

A terrible blizzard blasted outside, as Bishop Baraga lay in bed, breathing his last.

"Dear friends," he softly spoke, "I aim to be heaven bound." They asked,

"But how will you get there?"

"With the gentle caress of angel wings."

Biography of Frederic Baraga

Bishop Frederic Baraga, a missionary priest of the rugged territory of untamed Michigan and Lake Superior, was born in Dobernice, Slovenia, in 1797. He studied law before following the call to the priesthood. On December 31, 1830, he came to North America with a heart on fire for sharing the Gospel with the people there. For many years, he served the wild country alone, being the only priest for hundreds of miles.

The expanse of his territory and the harsh conditions of the winter climate challenged him, but did not sway him from his purpose. One winter season he trekked 690 miles on snowshoes, earning his nickname, "The Snowshoe Priest." In 1853 he was consecrated as bishop, and over time, moved the See of the Diocese from Sault Sainte Marie to Marquette, Michigan.

Bishop Baraga spoke several different European languages and mastered the "Anishinaabe" language of the Ottawa. He published a prayer book in that language, along with a grammar book and dictionary in the Chippewa language. He wrote about twenty books and kept a detailed diary of his travels and mission work. Saint John Neumann was so inspired by Baraga's missionary adventures, that he dedicated his life to mission work in the United States.

Bishop Baraga, acting on behalf of the Good Shepherd, often went out to save the lost ones. He snowshoed fifty-seven miles one way, through the winter woodlands, to baptize a dying child, before retracing his steps and returning home. Bishop Baraga was the heroic "Apostle of the Lakelands" bringing the Mass and the sacraments to the Ottawa and Chippewa people, the European immigrants, and the French Canadians. He met with trappers, traders, miners, explorers, both Catholic and non-Catholic. He catechized the people of the Great Lakes region for thirty-seven years, typically lacking the basic things necessary for survival, namely, hearty food and clothing appropriate for the harsh winter season. His burning desire to share the Gospel message was fueled by steady prayer and sacrifice.

Several places honor the memory of Bishop Baraga. In Michigan, a village, county, and state park bear his name, and the St. Peter Cathedral in Marquette is situated on Baraga Street. Between the villages of Baraga and L'Anse, a sixty-foot-tall copper statue shows the missionary priest with snowshoes in hand, casting his glance over the Keweenaw Bay. A granite cross now replaces Baraga's original wooden cross that celebrated his miraculous landing at the mouth of the Cross River (Schroeder, Minnesota). The Holy Name of Mary Proto-Cathedral, located in Sault Sainte Marie, houses a small museum displaying Bishop Baraga's Episcopal Chair along with his rocking chair, prayer books, and other personal items.

Bishop Baraga was treasured by the people of early America for his honesty and simplicity, respected for his grit and self-mastery, and remains as a model for all Christian men. In 2012 he was declared "Venerable" by Pope Benedict XVI.

Prayer for the Beatification of Bishop Frederic Baraga

O God,
thank You for the life
and holiness of Your servant,
Frederic Baraga.
I pray You will honor him
with the title of Saint.
He dedicated himself completely
to missionary activity
to make You known, loved, and served
by the people who You love.
As a man of peace and love,
Baraga brought peace and love
wherever he traveled.
Lord, grant Venerable Bishop Baraga
the grace of beatification.
We ask this in Christ's name.
Amen.

To report favors granted,
visit bishopbaraga.org

Or contact:
Baraga Association
615 S. Fourth Street
Marquette, MI 49855
(906) 227-9117

Heaven's Treasure

The Story of Venerable Father Samuel Mazzuchelli

"Samuel," his father questioned him, "why do you want to be a Dominican priest? Why not be a wise scholar, a great artist, or a wealthy businessman here in Italy?"

"A worldly career?" Samuel answered. "No. I will be a priest and go anywhere the work is great and difficult."

"But you could be rich!" his father begged.

"I'll help open the way for the gospel," Samuel replied, "and I'll share heaven's treasure."

Samuel followed the old Roman
road to the monastery at Faenza.
"Welcome," one of the brothers said,
waving from the door.
"We have a place for you!"
another friar chimed in.
Samuel got right to work.
He fetched water from the well,
tended the garden, and swept
the dusty floors. Every day, the brothers
sang and prayed and studied
the wise old books.
One day they said,
"Samuel, it's time you wear
the Dominican robe!"

As the long white tunic fell to his feet, he folded his hands in prayer saying,

"I am blessed with heaven's treasure!"

Samuel went to Rome and met Father Rese, a priest from a faraway shore.

"Come to America!" he pleaded. "Bishop Fenwick needs brave men who are willing to work hard and bring the gospel."

Samuel jumped up saying, "Send me!"

The priest replied, "So many people fill the untamed land. It's the poorest and largest diocese in the world."

"The place may be poor,"

Samuel said,

"but I'll bring heaven's treasure."

Samuel traveled through Italy,
climbing up and over the Alps.
He stayed in France until his ship
was set to sail.
The captain asked,
"Are you ready to cross the Atlantic?"
Samuel said, "Yes!
To open the way for the Gospel!"

After the ship docked in New York Harbor,
Samuel went by stagecoach
and riverboat to Cincinnati, Ohio.
There, Bishop Fenwick ordained
Samuel a priest.

"Father Samuel," the Bishop said,
"I'm sending you to Mackinac Island, Green
Bay settlement, and Sault Sainte Marie.
The Black Robes brought the
faith to the people there, years ago.
The northwest territory is
half the size of your homeland!
You'll be the only priest for hundreds of
miles, and I can give only my blessing."

"That is enough,"

Father Samuel said.

"I'm blessed with heaven's treasure."

On Mackinac Island, Madame la Framboise greeted him, saying, "We've been waiting for you! Our old church needs fixing, and our faith needs to be built up, too!"

Trappers and traders, immigrants and all of the people gathered for Mass in the Church of St. Anne.

"I'm off to Green Bay Settlement!"

Father Samuel said one day.

"I'll bring them heaven's treasure."

"Let's build the first church here, and name it for St. John the Evangelist!" Father Samuel said to the people of Green Bay. As he drew a cross in the dirt a man said, "Your white cassock will be ruined!"

"Not to worry!" the happy priest replied. "I'll be donning a black one from now on, with Bishop Fenwick's blessing."

An old woman chimed in, "Just like the Black Robes of long ago."

On his way back to Mackinac, Father Samuel sailed the waters of the bay, and stopped to see Father Baraga in Arbor Croche.

"Finally we meet!" he cried happily, shaking the other's hand.
The two missionaries prayed and talked for days, sharing stories of their adventures in the rugged land.

"By snowshoe and birch bark canoe,
we bring the gift of faith," Father Baraga said.

"Yes,"

Father Samuel replied,

"sharing heaven's treasure."

Father Samuel worked, helping to harvest wild rice in the autumn, tapping maple trees in the spring, and fishing on the frozen lake in the icy winter time. He learned and loved the ways of the people.

"I have something for you," he said, showing them a special prayer book. "In our language!" a young boy shouted.

"Talking with God and praising Him," the priest said, "is a share in heaven's treasure."

Under the leafy boughs of the golden oaks, Father Samuel set up an altar. He said to those kneeling nearby,

"Brothers and sisters, see how good God is, that he blesses us with such beauty: emerald green grass, blue sapphire sky, silvery shadows, and dancing diamonds from the sun."

He paused.

"All are glimpses of heaven's treasure."

Michael, a boy of the Menominee tribe, helped Father Samuel teach the faith. One day a friend asked him, "Why does this priest eat with us and sleep on the ground just as we do?"

Another asked, "Why does he treat us with such kindness?"

"He wants to share true joy,"

Michael replied,

"and it's found in heaven's treasure."

Father Samuel picked up his pen and wrote:

"Dear President Andrew Jackson, the people are being pushed out. Give them a share in the land,"

Father Samuel pleaded,

"for they share heaven's treasure."

Father Samuel's mission took him to the upper Mississippi River Valley. Irish immigrant miners, digging out lead ore, shouted to him, "Father Mazzuchelli! We'll call you Father Matthew Kelly! We're going to strike it rich!"

"All the wealth in the world,"

Father Samuel reminded them,

"will never compare to heaven's treasure."

Wherever Father Samuel stopped, a beautiful church seemed to grow up from the ground. St. Michael's in Galena, St. Raphael's in Dubuque, St. Gabriel's in Prairie du Chien!

"Each Catholic church,"

Father Samuel said,

"is a house for heaven's treasure."

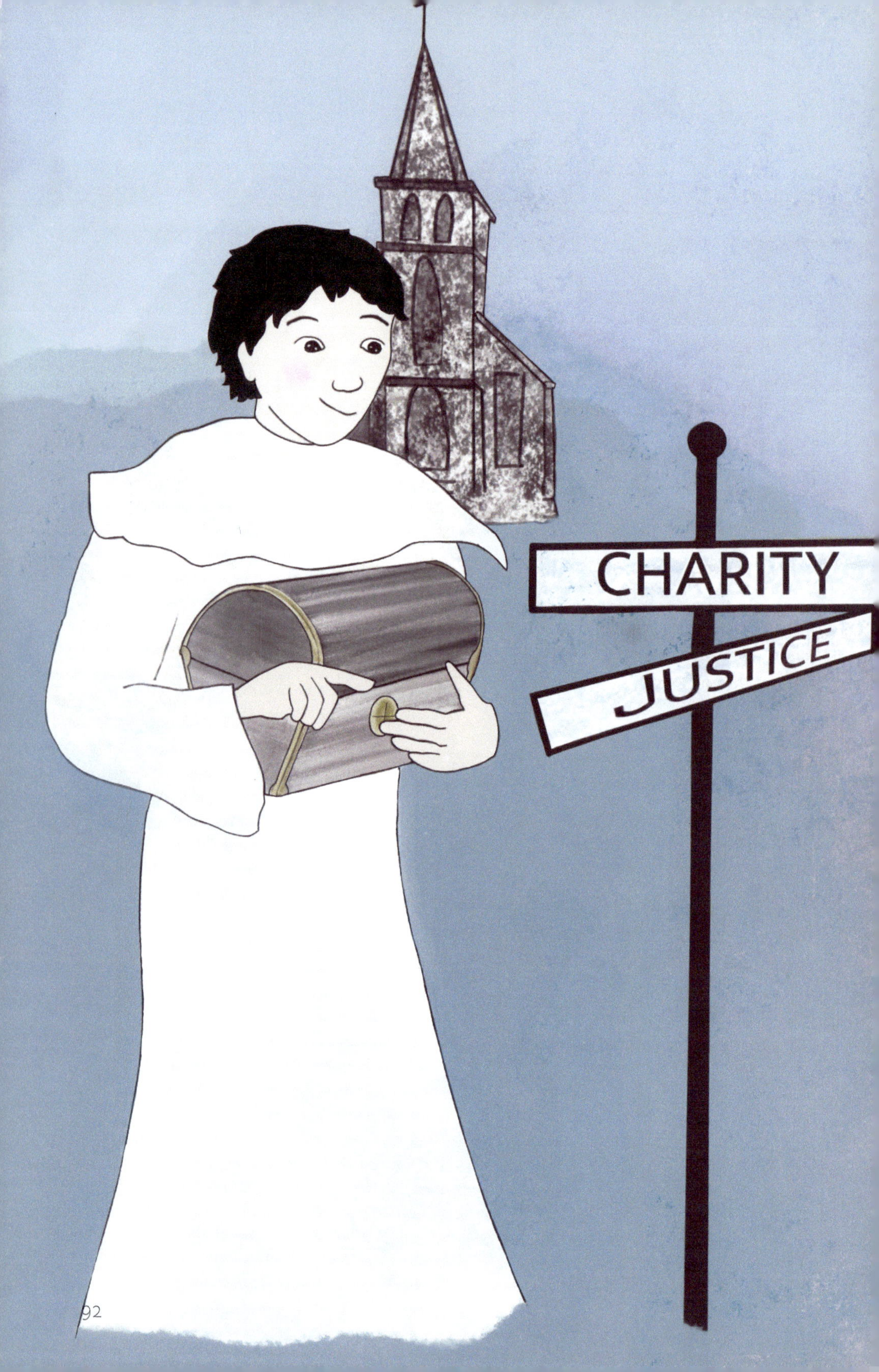
CHARITY
JUSTICE

People of Shullsburg, Wisconsin, following Father Samuel out the door of St. Matthew's Church, walked with him on the street named Peace, rounding the corners of Charity and Justice, then strolled down Friendship Lane.

"Blessed be all who walk in virtue,"

Father Samuel said,

"for this leads to heaven's treasure."

Father Samuel built a convent for the Dominican Sisters in Sinsinawa, Wisconsin. One day, while he was walking with the nuns, he stopped in the road.

"Who is he talking to?" one sister wondered, "he is speaking with such heavenly speech."

"Father Samuel," a second sister asked, "who are you talking with?"

"Dear sisters, there is great beauty in the world,"

Father Samuel replied,

"but none compares with heaven's treasure."

On a bitterly cold night,
someone knocked on his door, shouting,
"Father! Hurry! We need your blessing!"

Out the door the priest ran,
forgetting his coat,
but remembering heaven's treasure.

Over the next few days,
the frigid night's chill settled
deep within his bones.

"Father Samuel is sick!" a friend said,
"this was too much for him to take."

"I've given all I have to give,"

Father Samuel whispered,

"and I'm ready for heaven's treasure."

Biography of Samuel Mazzuchelli

Samuel Mazzuchelli was born in 1806 to a wealthy family in Milan, Italy. The big house he lived in as a child was so near to the cathedral, that he could see its spires poking up into the clouds. As a young boy, he dreamed of being a priest in the Dominican Order of Preachers, the religious order founded by St. Dominic de Guzman in 1216, but Samuel's father wished he would become a businessman or banker, as his other family members had done.

Samuel, desiring to share "the treasures of heavenly wisdom," stayed true to God's call, and in time, his father traveled with him to the monastery in Faenza, Italy, where he became a novice, a new member of the order, when he was seventeen years old. After two years, he received the white habit of St. Dominic. He went to Rome for more prayer and study, all the while becoming more ready to "set out for any place where the work is great and difficult" and, with God's help, to "open the way for the gospel."

Bishop Edward Fenwick of Cincinnati, Ohio, sent his vicar general, Father Frederick Rese to Rome, in search of brave men willing to come to the United States and be missionary priests in the northern part of his diocese, continuing the work that the Jesuits, the Black Robes, had begun generations before. Samuel set out for America, was ordained in Cincinnati in 1830, and from there went to settlements in the Northwest Territory, namely, Mackinac, Green Bay, and Sault Sainte Marie.

The Catholics in Mackinac were overjoyed at having a priest again. Father Samuel helped build up the church of St. Anne, and then went to Green Bay, founding the first Catholic church, St. John the Evangelist. He designed and helped construct more than twenty church buildings, established schools, was the architect for important civic buildings, and mapped out the streets of Shullsburg, Wisconsin, naming them after virtues. His missionary work stretched through Wisconsin, reaching into Illinois and Iowa.

Father Mazzuchelli found spiritual support in his friend and confessor, Father Frederic Baraga, who was also a missionary priest in the north. Like Father Baraga, Samuel wrote for the indigenous people, publishing a prayer book in the Winnebago language, and translating the New Testament and several school texts into the Menominee language. The first item printed in Wisconsin was his liturgical almanac, in the language of the Chippewa.

Samuel was involved in the government of the territory, speaking at Wisconsin's first legislative session. He wrote to President Andrew Jackson, defending the rights of the people. While ministering to the lead miners in the upper Mississippi valley region, the Irish affectionately nicknamed him "Matthew Kelly." He was a true friend to all.

He established the Dominican Sisters of Sinsinawa, Wisconsin. In Sinsinawa, there is a museum displaying his books and other personal things. Father Samuel had a strong devotion to the Blessed Virgin Mary, and one day, while traveling with some of the sisters, he had a vision of her. He died on February 23, 1864, and was proclaimed "Venerable" by Saint Pope John Paul II in 1993.

Prayer for the Beatification of Father Samuel Mazzuchelli, O.P.

Lord Jesus,
You called Your servant,
Samuel, even in early youth,
to leave home for a Dominican life
of charity in preaching Your Holy Gospel.
You gave him abundant graces
of Eucharistic love,
devotion to Your Holy Mother of Sorrows,
and a consuming zeal for souls.
Grant, we beseech You,
that his fervent love and labors for You
may become more widely known,
to a fruitful increase of Your Mystical Body,
to his exaltation and to our own
constant growth in devoted love of You,
Who with the Father and the Holy Spirit
live and reign one God, world without end.
Amen.

To report favors granted,
visit sinsinawa.org

Or contact:
Mazzuchelli Office
585 County Road Z.
Sinsinawa, WI 53824
(608) 748-4411

www.ingramcontent.com/pod-product-compliance
Lightning Source LLC
Chambersburg PA
CBHW042044290426
44109CB00001B/25